CUFF LINKS

BY SUSAN JONAS AND MARILYN NISSENSON

HARRY N. ABRAMS, INC., PUBLISHERS, NEW YORK

Editor: Harriet Whelchel
Designer: Carol Robson
with Gilda Hannah
Research Assistant: Agathe Berman

Library of Congress Cataloging-in-Publication Data

Jonas, Susan.
    Cuff links / by Susan Jonas and Marilyn Nissenson.
        p.   cm.
    Includes index.
    ISBN 0–8109–3168–0
    1. Cuff links—History.   I. Nissenson, Marilyn, 1939–
II. Title.
GT2282.J66   1991
391′.7—dc20   91–10154
                                                       CIP

Published in 1991 by Harry N. Abrams, Incorporated,
New York
A Times Mirror Company

Printed and bound in Japan

Authors' notes: Many of the cuff links pictured in this book are
shown larger than their actual size so that their imagery and
workmanship can be seen clearly.
    The authors wish to thank John Parnell, who did the principal
photography for this book, and Turnbull & Asser Ltd., which
provided the shirting fabric for the backgrounds of most of the
photographs.

Page 1: Porcelain and 18-carat gold. English, 1880s. Kentshire
Galleries, New York

Page 2: Calibré-cut rubies, diamonds, and platinum. Van Cleef
& Arpels, French, 1936. Van Cleef & Arpels Museum
Invisibly set calibré-cut diamonds, sapphires, and rubies are a
staple of Art Deco jewelry. In the mid-1930s Van Cleef devised
invisible settings, and for a time their patent prohibited other
jewelers from copying the technique. It proved so popular,
however, that it soon appeared everywhere.
    The edges of the calibré-cut stones are grooved precisely to
slide into the metal tracks of a tiny metal lattice, which will be
completely hidden by the stones it supports. Each fitted stone
can be mounted to fill or follow any shape or space, including
curves.
    This pair, which has 216 calibré-cut rubies and 72 pavé
diamonds, is among the most famous baton-shaped links ever
made. The pairs on page 92 are variations.

Page 5: Eighteen-carat gold and enamel, depicting Punch and
Judy puppets. English, 1880. Tender Buttons, New York

CONTENTS

INTRODUCTION

Diamond dress suite, one cuff-link-bar fitting inscribed WALLIS, 19.6.35, the other DAVID, 23.6.35; two of the three button fittings inscribed, respectively, HOLD TIGHT and E 7/5/35. Cartier, London, 1935. Private Collection

This dress suite was given to Edward, Prince of Wales, by Wallis Simpson during their courtship. Estimated to bring $10,000 at the 1987 sale of the Windsors' jewels, the suite sold for $440,000, the highest price recorded for a single dress suite.

Opposite: Onyx with diamonds and calibré-cut rubies. French, 1920s. Private Collection

In 1935 Wallis Simpson ordered a pair of diamond cuff links from Cartier on New Bond Street in London. As she .requested, the links were made of brilliant-cut diamonds pavé-set in platinum, with baguette diamonds that formed the initials E and W. They were accompanied by studs and buttons inscribed HOLD TIGHT and dated 7/5/35, the day on which Mrs. Simpson gave them to her lover, Edward, the Prince of Wales. A year later, by then Edward VIII, he gave Wallis a ruby and diamond bracelet made by Van Cleef & Arpels, also inscribed HOLD TIGHT. The words expressed their feelings while Edward agonized over renouncing his throne for the woman he loved.

Through the years, Wallis Simpson, the Duchess of Windsor, collected necklaces, brooches, earrings, rings, and other remarkable jewels. Many were gifts from her husband. The duke loved to see the duchess wearing jewels, but with the exception of one or two discreet rings on his little finger, he seldom wore any jewelry other than cuff links.

Most men own at least one pair of cuff links for formal wear. Fathers traditionally pass them on to sons. Bridegrooms give them to ushers. Presidents of countries and corporations hand them out to ambassadors, clients, and faithful retainers. Any man riffling through his top dresser drawer can lay his hands on a pair of cuff links with a monogram, family crest, regimental colors, birthdate, or corporate or school seal. Sometimes the reference is obscure, and often only one link remains.

Some men are passionate collectors. The most obsessed can change their cuff links every day for more than a year without wearing the same pair twice. As Fabienne Falluel, a curator at the Musée de la Mode et du Costume, points out, cuff links are among the few items of men's jewelry that are considered socially acceptable. Like watches, belt buckles, and tie pins, they are functional and therefore regarded as "manly."

Such a puritanical attitude is not always true of other cultures or other times. Tribesmen in Africa and the South Pacific and princes in the Indian subcontinent, for example, have traditionally worn lavish jewelry. In the sixteenth century, Cosimo de Medici, the epitome of Florentine high society, covered himself with jewels, and Henry VIII of England had emeralds and rubies sewn into his clothes. The allure of jewelry for men in the West has always been more widespread than is commonly acknowledged. In 1934 a fashion writer asserted in *Men's Wear,* a journal for the retail trade, that "there can be no doubt that men like jewelry. Given the chance and if fashion indicated, they would wear earrings or nose rings."

Most people assume that cuff links date back to the sixteenth or seventeenth century. Who can imagine Restoration fops or powdered courtiers at Versailles without gaudy jewels at their wrists? But it was not until the end of the eighteenth century that

The Duke of Windsor, photographed by Hoyningen-Huene a few days before the duke's marriage to Wallis Simpson on June 3, 1937.

cuff links as we now know them appeared. The evolution of these functional yet elegant accessories was determined by the history of the man's shirt.

Men have worn shirtlike garments since the invention of woven fabric in the fifth millennium BC. Although cut and construction have altered through the centuries, the basic shape of the shirt remains today: a tunic, opening in the front, with long or short sleeves and some kind of collar. Worn next to the skin and washable, the shirt helped prevent outer clothing from being soiled by close contact with the body. The shirt also protected the skin from a rougher or heavier outer garment by extending beyond it at the neck and wrists where chafing was likely to occur.

The shirt could be worn without a jacket for manual labor and for informal occasions. In warm climates it was and is acceptable to omit the jacket for dressier events. But for most of its history, the shirt has functioned as an undergarment, and any attempt to sanction the public exposure of shirtsleeves has been anathema to the guardians of "taste," even in the twentieth century. For example, the New York *Sun* on June 1, 1901, deplored the fact that men were reported to have abandoned their suit jackets on a blistering Kansas City summer day:

> Thermometers may lie or tell the truth. Why should anybody care? Compared with the poor devils in the stoke room, you are as ice to fire. . . . A man without a coat on has no business in hotels or restaurants or offices other than his own. . . . A man in a shirt-waist can't be anything else than a "slouch." He will be punished by copious perspirations. . . . It was the coat that bound him to civilization.

After the late Middle Ages, the visible areas of the shirt—the neck, wrists, and front—became decorative features of male fashion, complementing the main outer garment with frills and embroidery. The precursors of cuffs first appeared in the early 1500s as tiny ruffles at the wristband of the shirtsleeve. An inventory of a nobleman's wardrobe from the time of Henry VIII lists four shirts with bands and ruffles of silver. Ruffles were sometimes an inch wide, sometimes flowing, and sometimes folded back, as seen in portraits by Frans Hals and Anthony van Dyck. Those elaborately embroidered seventeenth-

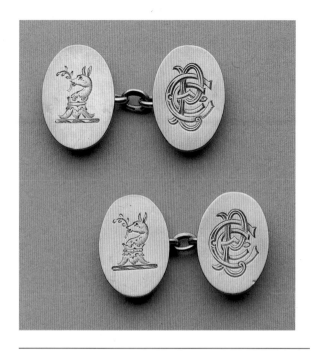

Eighteen-carat gold, inscribed C. E. P., engraved with a hart's head. English, c. 1910. Collection John Pym

Cuff links engraved with a monogram or family crest are a common gift from father to son. This pair, made for Charles Evelyn Pym and engraved with the family crest, has been passed on for several generations.

Eighteen-carat gold, engraved with the insignia of the Tilers and Bricklayers Company, a guild first incorporated in 1568. English, c. 1940. Collection John Pym

One gold sleeve link with filigree. English, probably late 17th century. Ted Donohoe, London

Excavated at Bury St. Edmunds in 1989, this is one of the earliest sleeve fasteners extant.

One silver sleeve link, embossed with a profile portrait of Queen Anne and the initials AR [ANNA REGINE]. English, early 18th century. Museum of London

century neck ruffs were eventually modified to become recognizable shirt collars, and the fancy sleeve ruffles evolved into cuffs.

At first wristbands had a small opening on either side through which a thin ribbon or string was passed and then tied to hold the sleeve closed. (A similar string or ribbon used to tie up the shirt collar was the forerunner of the cravat.) Men realized only gradually that closing the wristband gave them a chance to flaunt their wealth. Even Louis XIV, who owned a set of one hundred and four diamond buttons and wore forty-eight studs on one of his waistcoats, probably wore tiny colored strings at the end of his shirtsleeves.

Although cuff strings were worn until the early nineteenth century, in the last years of Louis's reign, fashionable men began to wear pairs of identical or similar buttons — joined by a short chain — to fasten their sleeves. The *London Gazette* of 1684 referred to a pair of "cuff buttons" set with diamonds, and two years later the same journal described a pair of enameled gold "sleeve buttons." (For several hundred years, the terms would be used interchangeably. Even today the French phrase is *bouton de manchette,* or "sleeve button.") Many experts believe that the oldest sleeve fastener extant is a single gold link with filigree, discovered in 1989 in Suffolk, England, that probably dates from the late seventeenth century.

Elaborate wrist ruffles, falling over the hands, continued to be worn for court appearances and other formal affairs until the end of the eighteenth century, while the sleeve of an everyday shirt ended in a simple band closed with a single button or linked pair of buttons. Country magistrates and other gentry with a flair for fashion might choose decorated buttons rather than those of a plain, serviceable design. For example, Lord George Greville, the son of the Earl of Warwick, seems to be wearing gold sleeve buttons in a 1754 portrait by Sir Joshua Reynolds.

The eighteenth century was the age of painted miniatures, and a popular motif for buttons of all kinds was expressed in polychrome portraits of loved ones or persons of distinction. Among the earliest sleeve fasteners is a set in the Victoria and Albert Museum collection: four buttons with the faces of four ruddy German ladies wearing white cloth bonnets. Nobody knows who they were or if one gentleman loved all four.

Several surviving pairs of eighteenth-century sleeve buttons are made of paste—a glass composition used for imitation gemstones—on a silver base, sometimes inscribed with the initials of the owner and his lady. A more elaborate crystal pair in the Museum of London reveals a portrait of a man on one button linked to the portrait of his wife on the other. The double-sided nature of cuff links lent itself naturally to paired wedding portraits, a genre of Western painting dating from the Renaissance.

Finally, by the mid-nineteenth century, the modern shirtsleeve cuff had evolved. It was sometimes a simple two-to-three-inch band—the so-called single or barrel cuff—or sometimes folded over, which in the early twentieth century came to be known as the French cuff. (No one can pinpoint the origin of this English and American usage; the French themselves say *poignet mousquetaire*, or "musketeer's cuff," preserving the memory of the cuff's antecedent as a ruffle at a seventeenth-century dandy's wrist.)

Nineteenth-century collars, cuffs, and shirtfronts were almost always stiff. Starch, which had been

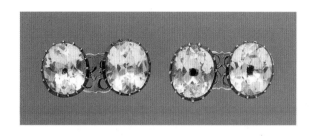

White paste in silver with original links. English, mid-18th century. Harvey & Gore, London

A glass composition, paste can be cut in a multitude of shapes more easily than diamonds can. The 1700s were the great age of paste, which was worn interchangeably with diamonds, despite the disparity in cost between them. By the mid-1800s, however, paste was used almost exclusively to imitate ordinary diamonds and was therefore no longer considered prestigious or chic.

One silver link with rock crystal over painted miniature portraits on paper depicting Prince Charles Edward and Princess Louise of Stolberg. English, early 18th century. Museum of London

around since the sixteenth century, was popular because it accentuated the formality of dress that Victorians found so desirable.

Gentlemen proclaimed their status by wearing shirts with collars and cuffs of the finest, whitest, most perishable material, which implied that they owned enough linen to change at least once a day. But working-class men or office clerks who owned one or two shirts could keep up appearances only with detachable collars and cuffs. A columnist for *Men's Wear* advised readers in 1902 that although "there is a remarkable growth in the popularity of the attached cuff, the call for attached cuffs will never equal that for detached ones." The New York *Sun* felt otherwise:

> We hold that a starched shirt bosom and collar will keep a man of the right temperament cooler than all the substitutes of limper fabric. As to the "detach-able" cuffs . . . they are an abomination. The cuffs should not be divorced from the shirt. When they are soiled the shirt is soiled.

Because men wore starched shirts, manufacturers sought a sleeve fastener that could be passed more easily through a stiff cuff than a button could. The most common solution was a metal chain or link fastener—hence the popularity of the term "cuff link." (The terms "sleeve button" and "cuff button" persisted in use, however, until the early twentieth century.) A variation was the flexible chain link, which expanded under tension when the sleeves were pushed up above the elbows. Some fasteners came in two separate pieces, one having a small projection and the other a matching depression, which were pressed together like a collar stud. Other links were

Eighteen-carat gold, moss agate, and garnets. English, late 18th century. A La Vieille Russie, New York

joined by levers or swivels. Especially popular in America were dumbbell designs—the front and back joined by a rigid but gently curved shank.

Early in the Victorian era, links were usually made of gold, silver, or ivory. After the California gold rush of 1848 and subsequent discoveries in the Yukon, South Africa, and Siberia, more precious metal was available to meet the growing demand. One reason so much jewelry from the nineteenth century survives—although frequently it was broken up and reassembled—is that it didn't have to be melted down to make new pieces.

As a rule, Victorian links were simple in design and conformed to middle-class taste. This simplicity was a by-product of the Industrial Revolution. Steam-driven stamping machines made possible the mass production of the faces and fasteners of ordi-

Eighteen-carat yellow-and-white-gold cuff buttons with agate cameos, in fitted original box. Cartier, French, c. 1880. Cartier Museum

The box is stamped 9, BOULEVART DES ITALIENS, indicating that the links were made before Cartier moved to the Rue de la Paix in Paris in 1899 and before the spelling of *boulevard* was standardized.

nary links, and electro-plating (fusing a coat of gold or silver to a base metal by means of an electric current) was invented in the 1860s. Cuff links became a staple commodity of London jewelers like Child & Child and E. W. Streeter or manufacturers like Cropp & Farr, who developed that specialty within the Birmingham, England, steel industry.

In America, George Krementz, a Newark, New Jersey, jeweler and inventor, bought a machine that had made cartridge shells during the Civil War. In the 1880s he patented an adaptation of it for the manufacture of collar buttons and one-piece cuff links. Parts that had been made separately and soldered together could now be stamped out whole. For a time Krementz & Co. cornered the collar-button market and was one of the largest producers of gold beam-and-post (a variant of the dumbbell) links.

Other American cuff-link manufacturers such as Carrington or Larter, Elcox & Co. clustered on Maiden Lane in New York and in Philadelphia and Providence. Some firms published their own catalogues for the retail trade; others manufactured links for better-known jewelers like Tiffany & Co. The 1878 Tiffany *Blue Book* featured "Presents for Gentlemen: Sleeve buttons—gold, stone, mosaic, enamels, carved crystals, and cameos" at prices ranging from less than $20 to more than $300. The Bloomingdale Brothers' *Illustrated Catalogue* for 1886 offered a pair of "very neat rolled gold sleeve buttons for 25¢ per pair." Other rolled and plated gold links fetched as much as 69, 79, and even 89 cents the pair.

Everyone in the middle and upper classes wore cuff links from the mid-nineteenth century on. Entire lines of cuff links were marketed expressly for women. In 1900 S. F. Myers, a well-known New York retail jeweler, advertised "Ladies' Waist Sets"—a pair of cuff links and three stud buttons—at prices ranging from $1.50 for a set in rolled gold to $13.75 for one in solid gold with inlaid pearls. Gibson Girls and suffragettes wore them, as did office clerks. Even chambermaids and cooks like Mrs. Bridges in the British television series *Upstairs Downstairs* wore links in their starched white shirts; one Englishman now in his seventies retains some slight aversion to cuff links because he associates them with a hated nanny.

As the Victorian era unfolded, more people became aware of fashion. Increased wealth, the opportunity to travel, affordable manufactured goods, and the growth of illustrated magazines showing how social leaders dressed all stimulated a demand for the latest in brooches, stomachers, earrings, tiaras, buckles, pendants, hair ornaments, lockets, and bangles. Men kept apace with cravat pins, walking sticks, and cuff links. Style became commercialized, often changing from season to season, year to year. Diana Scarisbrick, a British jewelry historian, writes:

> It used to be said that a Victorian jewelry fashion lasted just long enough for the lady of the house to find her maid wearing a one-and-sixpenny version of it. This is a simplification: some styles were evergreen and never out of fashion for long; others were so crazy or tasteless that they did not survive the season. Between these two extremes many fashions came and went.

Victorian imperialism brought Burmese rubies, Kashmiri sapphires, cat's-eyes from southwest Africa, green demantoid garnets from Siberia, opals from Australia, and, above all, South African diamonds to the Western world. Women wore the stones immediately; men accepted them gradually. Ever since Beau Brummell, the tastemaker of Regency England, had declared the height of masculine elegance to be a simple, unembellished blue coat, prevailing fashion had dictated that women should wear jewels and men should provide them. Modest diamond links and studs were permissible with evening

Eighteen-carat gold, with emeralds and enamel. Indian, late 19th century. Tender Buttons, New York

clothes, but until the end of the nineteenth century only the most self-confident man ventured out in cuff links emblazoned with precious stones.

As the nineteenth century drew to a close, artists and designers developed stylistic imperatives in reaction to the previous generation's taste. There was a fever of competing or complimentary design movements, each with its own ideology and aesthetic, known variously as Arts and Crafts, Art Nouveau, Jugendstil, and Wiener Werkstätte. These design philosophies were embodied in objects as diverse as furniture, wallpaper, clothing, utensils, and all manner of jewelry, including, of course, cuff links. The man who a decade earlier wore only mother-of-pearl links might now choose a pair made of translucent enamels, sinuous metalwork, or a combination of glass and other "lesser materials" with precious metals and stones.

By the beginning of the twentieth century, the

fashion of the period that came to be known as Edwardian was epitomized by the personal style of the new British monarch, King Edward VII. He and his family set the standard of the day for the well-dressed man. According to *The American Tailor and Cutter*, Edward's son, Prince George, was known as " 'Collars and Cuffs,' from his lavish display of these most important adjuncts to the male toilet," and George's brother, Prince Eddie, "by no means despises a close attention to particulars of costume, and in its consideration he must spend no few of his waking hours."

According to the Paris *Herald,* when King Edward arrived at Marienbad for the cure, his presence attracted "swarms of young dandies from Berlin, Budapest, Vienna, and other cities, as well as numerous tailors and outfitters, all intent upon obtaining hints as to the latest fashions from 'The First Gentleman of Europe.'" For daytime Edward favored easy-fitting light gray or brown suits with a contrasting hat. He loved bright colors; at every opportunity he wore red neckties, red socks, and red bands on his straw hats. His formal cuff links included a Fabergé pair of bright red enamel with rubies and diamonds.

During Victoria's heyday, a white or a conservatively striped shirt with a white collar had been the only correct choice for a gentleman. (Colored shirts with colored collars were associated with the laboring classes, or "blue-collar" workers.) By Edward's time, colored shirtings with white collars had become acceptable for daytime wear, especially in summer. Cuff links of brightly colored enamels and semiprecious stones were an attractive accessory. A *Men's Wear* reporter noted in 1905 that

in the haberdashery, the general effect is of clashing and flashing golds, silvers, oranges, purples, flaming crimsons and cardinals, peacock and ultramarine blues. . . . To be absolutely correct, [the well-dressed man's] underwear must be pink, his suspenders sky blue, his socks purple and his pajamas and waistcoat as well so "stunning" that whether dressed for day parade or slumber, the chromatic scheme of his apparel is kaleidoscopic.

A year later the same paper reported that cuff links made of American stones not previously considered valuable were now coming into prominence. Aquamarine was worn with pale blue and green shirt fabric, topaz with yellow and brown, garnet with various shades of red and other wintry tones, andalusite with plaids and checks, sodalite with delft blues, rutilated quartz with champagne-colored materials, and amethyst with lavendar. The variety, *Men's Wear* concluded, was good for business:

> The fact that many fashion leaders have adopted the newly popular stones serves further to strengthen their position with the public. As women are also very much implicated in the style, the vogue looks promising, indeed. To consistently carry out the color matching idea a man must own a number of sets and keep adding to his jewelry purchase as often as he adopts a new shade effect.

By the Edwardian Age, European trendsetters regularly wore links set with glittering precious stones for formal dress. In America, where fashion lagged behind the Continent, *The Sartorial Art Journal* wrote in 1908 that "anything more than plain pearl studs and sleeve links is regarded as the

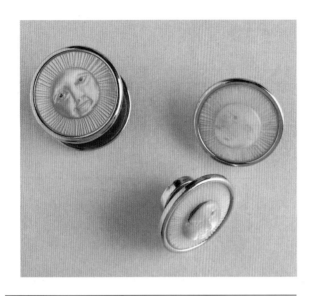

Mother-of-pearl buttons. Probably French, 19th century. Made into cuff links in 1949. Collection James Pendleton

attire of the 'bounder,' and to wear diamonds stamps one at once as *noveaux riche [sic].*"

Not till after World War I were American men as eager as their European counterparts to wear gemstones. The hedonism of the Jazz Age, which flaunted prewar social conventions, found expression in the universally popular dazzle of Art Deco design. *Men's Wear* wrote in 1923, "Never before in Paris has there been such a craze for wearing jeweled sleeve links as at the moment." The trend was reinforced by the appearance of the white evening jacket, which made its debut in Palm Beach in 1931. With it many men preferred colored cuff links—rubies, emeralds, sapphires. Dress suites of these precious stones were so popular that they were copied immediately in semiprecious versions or even plain glass.

The fascination with male presentation between the wars can be attributed directly to the Duke of Windsor, who has been called the greatest arbiter of taste in the twentieth century. He sanctioned the double-breasted chalk-striped suit for street wear and invented the Windsor knot. He also popularized plus fours, tweed suits, and suede shoes for lounging about on country weekends. Although the duke habitually wore cuff links, many of which he had inherited from his father and grandfather, his fashion legacy was casualness in dress, which eventually made cuff links fall from favor.

"The sport shirt has played havoc with a lot of incidentals in men's wear. The widespread adoption of this shirt, not only by sportsmen, but by comfort seekers who wear it during business hours, must have removed a sizeable slice from the collar business and put a crimp in cuff link wearing," *Men's Wear* reported in 1923. "Inasmuch as the most popular of these shirts have barrel cuffs which close with a sewed-on pearl button, it dispenses with the wearing of links."

The quest for comfort and ease of dress led to the return of the unstarched cuff in the 1920s. Wearing links became an option rather than an obligation for the first time in nearly one hundred years. Fashionable men could appear in daytime without links, and, increasingly, men who chose to wear them were upper class or aspiring to be.

During the Depression and certainly for the duration of World War II, fashion and jewelry were a low priority for most men. But they reappeared as embodiments of American confidence and prosperity in the years just after the war. In 1948 *Esquire* pronounced the "Bold Look for the Dominant Male:

Ten-carat gold-filled, with porcelain, opal, enamel, and uranium ore. Destino Ltd., American, 1958–70.
Collection Ralph Destino

... His offices touch on two oceans, with branches midway between. Our man has learned to fly thousands of miles as casually as he once travelled across town, and to keep his feet on the ground while reaching decisions with his head in the air. His role is modern, demanding; his appearance at the airport must be 100% perfect the minute they feather the props." The postwar man wore "richly coordinated jewelry," consisting of cigarette case, lighter, cuff links, tie tack, key chain, ID bracelet, money clip, and gold-studded wallet. He wore a "bold look" shirt and "bigger, chunkier" cuff links with his gray flannel suit. His links could be either the real thing or costume jewelry, which was all the rage.

Twelve-carat gold. Paul Flato, American, 1930s. Private
Collection

In the 1930s, Coco Chanel had made the bold
scale and frankly acknowledged fakery of costume
jewelry acceptable to the most fashionable women.
After World War II, American designers of men's
accessories followed suit, mass-producing cuff links
of nonprecious metals and imitation or semiprecious
stones made to keep up with the latest trends. For
spring 1955, Swank, the world's largest manufac-
turer of men's jewelry, advertised "Fashion-tone
jewelry . . . Tie Klips & Cuff Links to match or mix
with the new pastel colors in shirts." The buyer could
choose the "Rex Set"—a silverplate lion's head on a
background of pink enamel—or the "Spartan
Set"—a silver gladiator on a field of mint green.

By the late 1950s, Destino Ltd., one of the lead-
ing manufacturers of male accessories, had an inventory of fourteen thousand designs for 12-carat-
gold-filled and silver cuff links; the firm produced six
hundred variations every year, replacing two hundred of them every spring and another four hundred
every fall. Each pair came with a provenance: the
information accompanying Wedgwood jasper-blue
and white sculpted discs included the Wedgwood
hallmark and the initials of the original designer;
another pair were made of colored sandstone "from
the Ellenburger formation, Pecos County, Texas,
geologic age Cambrian—4000 million years old!"
The purchaser of gold-filled nuggets with traces of
uranium was reassured by a certificate from the
Atomic Energy Commission that there was no dan-
ger from radiation.

All fourteen thousand Destino cuff-link designs
featured the same prosaic back. Americans have
usually preferred single-face links with a hinged
back or other simple fastener to the double-face
European models because they are easier to put on.
Ralph Destino, formerly head of the company that
bore his name and now chairman of the board of
Cartier, Inc., New York, says, "If you ask fifty American men to show the backs of their sleeves, you'll see
fifty identical fasteners. European cuff links are
more intricate, but some are so hard to get on that
you need a valet, a wife, or three hands."

In the late 1960s, traditional menswear in general
and cuff links in particular were eclipsed by tie-dyed
shirts, glass beads, and Nehru jackets from "swing-
ing London." For a time fashion seemed dominated
by Carnaby Street and the Woodstock generation.
Even after the hippies disappeared in the mid-
seventies, "no one" but the most debonair wore cuff
links. Many beautiful antique pairs were converted
into earrings.

The Reagan era brought back the pleasures of conspicuous consumption. In July 1989 *DNR,* the Fairchild newspaper for the menswear trade, proclaimed: "Cuff Links Comeback Continues: Cuff links are in the midst of a renaissance. . . . The marketplace is poised and ready to offer a greater and superior variety of cuff links, along with tie bars and belt buckles, to provide elegant furnishings that provide the finishing touch for the well-heeled man." In September 1990 *GQ* reported that the cuff link "has come roaring back."

Cuff links continue to fascinate designers because of the challenges they pose. They are among the few pieces of jewelry with size constraints that dominate design. The standard cuff offers very little room for display, especially since the jacket covers all but a narrow strip of it. The links themselves must lie smartly on the sleeve. And whether there are four identical faces, four differing ones, or two faces with unadorned backs, the images must relate to each other aesthetically.

The ingenuity of designers can be tested in improbable situations. Eddie Duchin, the 1930s bandleader, was entertaining jeweler Paul Flato in his hotel suite before a society ball. As he was putting on his shirt studs, Duchin was astonished to see that Flato was wearing an unusual pair of cuff links. Flato explained that, while dressing for dinner, he could not lay his hands on a single pair of links. Pressed for time, he rustled up two brass nuts and bolts, inserted them in his cuffs, and went on his way. Duchin asked for an identical pair made up in gold, which he eventually passed on to his son, Peter. Flato made several other pairs that are as highly prized among collectors as the most luxurious Art Deco dress suite. Whether paste or diamond, whimsical or classic, cuff links provide a hundred ways for a man to wear his art on his sleeve.

A VICTORIAN POTPOURRI

Green-stained ivory and gold. Designed by Sir Edward Burne-Jones, made by Child & Child, English, 1880s. Wartski, London

The Pre-Raphaelite painter and jewelry designer Sir Edward Burne-Jones preferred stained ivory to precious stones. The heart, a symbol of love, was one of his favorite decorative devices. He designed a similar pair of cuff links for his own use.

Opposite: White and *guilloché* red enamel, diamond, and 18-carat gold. English, c. 1850. Private Collection

Victorian jewelry reflected the romanticism, love of antiquity, and sentimentality that characterized most of the nineteenth century. Anything eclectic or unusual could be exploited for design. Recent discoveries in archaeology stimulated a fascination with Greek, Etruscan, and Egyptian styles that led jewelers to copy the goldwork of ancient craftsmen and revive neglected techniques of enameling on metal. An idealized past created by Sir Walter Scott fueled the Gothic revival. Even before Commodore Matthew Perry entered Tokyo Bay, Oriental motifs influenced both popular culture and high art. When Queen Victoria was proclaimed Empress of India, Indian jewelry became the vogue.

Victorian sentimentality was personified by the Queen herself, who wore widow's weeds for forty years after the death of Prince Albert. Her impressionable countrymen marked their own bereavements with elaborate costumes and complete sets of mourning jewelry made of anything black: enamel, jet, onyx, glass, cast iron, papier-mâché, vulcanite, and petrified oak. The memory of dead or absent loved ones was also evoked by jewelry woven from their hair. Such jewelry became so desirable that entire lines of earrings, necklaces, watch chains, and cuff links made from hair were mass produced.

During the day, the Victorian gentleman wore a dark frock coat or the increasingly popular jacket without tails, light trousers, waistcoat, soft cravat or necktie, top hat, cane, and gold or enameled cuff links. Fashionable men might choose one-of-a-kind links created by Giuliano, Wiese, Cartier, Fabergé, Tiffany, and other master jewelers who catered to their wives. For evening, white tie and tails were *de rigueur*, with cuff links and studs of precious or semiprecious stones. By the 1880s electric lights enhanced the sparkle of faceted gems and brought up the subtlety of colorless links made of mother-of-pearl, opals, and moonstones.

Aristocrats determined fashion. In Europe affluent doctors, solicitors, and stockbrokers were consulted professionally, but, as Lady Warwick, a prominent London social figure, pronounced, they could "never [be invited] to luncheon or dinner." Even in America, where social position was more flexible, the nouveaux riches aspired to live and dress like dukes. Although the personal style of the queen was dowdy, the patricians who ruled in her behalf, and the upper-middle classes who sought to emulate them, loved to display their formal and impressive jewelry whenever possible.

Turquoise, amethyst, chrysoprase, and carnelian scarabs; rose diamonds; and gold. Fabergé, Russian, 1880s. A La Vieille Russie, New York

Indian turquoise and rose diamonds. English, c. 1850. S. J. Phillips, London

Eighteen-carat gold, with raised head of Medusa in Etruscan style. Italian, c. 1870. Private Collection

Above left: Mixed metals. Late 19th century. Collection Gilbert Jonas. *Above right:* Eighteen-carat gold and mixed metals in the Japanese style. Tiffany & Co., probably American, 1880s. Private Collection

The links on the left were probably made in the West from Japanese buttons. They are examples of Shakudo work, a Japanese technique using an alloy of 75 to 90 percent copper and pure gold. While jewelers in the West were fascinated with Japanese motifs and Japanese metalwork—especially the fabulous swords—the Japanese themselves did not make or wear jewelry.

Mosaic set in 18-carat gold. Italian, 1870s.
Private Collection

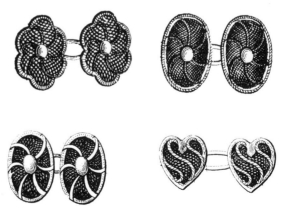

Cuff-link designs from a 19th-century English catalogue of hair jewelry. Collection Joyce Jonas

The artistic arrangement of human hair in jewelry dates from Georgian times. It became a fashion craze in the 1800s. Because horsehair could be substituted by unscrupulous jewelers, young women were advised to learn how to trim and braid their own locks before commissioning a keepsake for lovers or friends.

Eighteen-carat gold, with champlevé enamel, in a fitted original box. Carlo and Arthur Giuliano, English, late 19th century. Wartski, London

Italian art jewelers led the Victorian revival of interest in Greek, Etruscan, Gothic, and Renaissance styles. The Giuliano family moved from Naples to England, opening a business in Piccadilly in the early 1870s. Not content simply to copy antique pieces, they created new designs in the ancient manner. Their workshop was noted for meticulous craftsmanship, elegant enameling, and delicacy of design.

Carnelian intaglios framed in 18-carat gold. Mellilo, Italian, late 19th century. Private Collection

Giacinto Melillo (1846–1915) was a Neapolitan goldsmith especially skilled at reproducing ancient jewelry.

Cast gold. Wiese, French, c. 1870. Hancocks & Co., London

Silver and niello buttons, each with a view of the Kremlin, mounted as cuff links. Russian, 19th century. A La Vieille Russie, New York

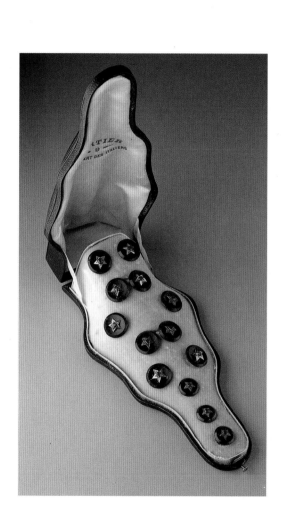

Lapis lazuli, ruby, and vermeil dress suite, in fitted original box. Cartier, French, c. 1895. Cartier Collection

Enamel, ruby, and diamond dress
suite. English, c. 1890.
Private Collection

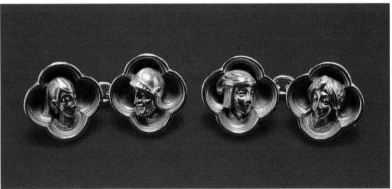

Eighteen-carat gold, with four
faces said to represent Abélard and
Héloïse, Lancelot and Guinevere.
Wiese, French, c. 1865. Collection
Malcolm Carr

This pair with portraits of famous
lovers was a wedding gift to the present owner from his wife.

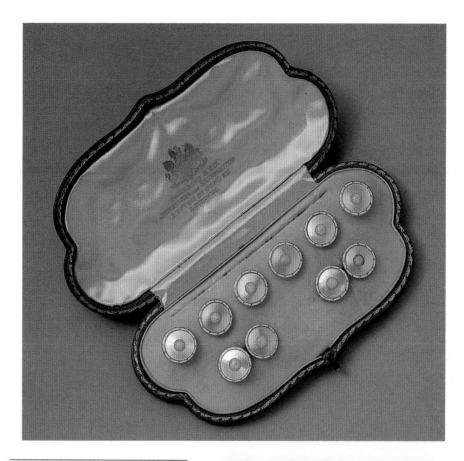

Above: Mother-of-pearl and White Cliffs—opal dress suite, in original fitted box. English, 1890s. Hancocks & Co., London

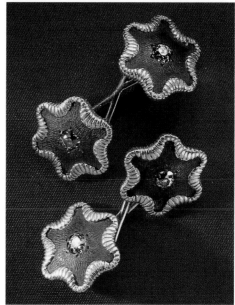

Gunmetal, diamond, and 18-carat gold. Tiffany & Co., American, 1880s. Private Collection

ART NOUVEAU:
Sinuousness and Sensuality

Sketch from Tiffany & Co. design book. c. 1900.
Tiffany Archives

Opposite: Enamel and 18-carat gold. European,
c. 1900. Private Collection

Although Queen Victoria lived until 1901, in the last decades of her life, innovations in art, technology, and science shook the complacency of her era. Launched in the mid-1880s, the design movement known as Art Nouveau rejected the imitative styles of the previous generation and adopted an aesthetic based on sinuous lines, virtuoso techniques, references to nature, and exotic imagery. By 1900 the "new art" flourished throughout Europe.

Among the influences on Art Nouveau was the British Arts and Crafts movement, inspired by John Ruskin and William Morris, who resisted what they believed were the excesses of industrial society. Archibald Knox and fellow Arts and Crafts designers made handcrafted objects for Liberty & Co. based on preindustrial Celtic and pagan motifs. Related movements in Germany, Austria, and America sought to bring a new purity to mass-produced objects for the growing middle class.

Jewelers of all the aesthetic movements used precious, semiprecious, and nonprecious gems and metals side by side. They believed the design of an object was more important than the intrinsic value of its materials. They loved milky, soft-looking pearls, cat's-eyes, and moonstones. Opals were popular, despite the persistence of an old superstition that they brought bad luck.

Art Nouveau jewelers perfected the art of enameling in delicate, naturalistic colors. *Plique-à-jour* enamels are produced when colored glass in powdered form is placed between metal walls and then fired, creating a transparent effect similar to stained glass. In cloisonné enameling, the wire walls are attached to a metal backing; the cell walls separate the colors in the finished piece and are an integral part of the design. In champlevé pieces, the areas to be enameled are carved out of the background metal; the enamels are laid down and fired in several layers. In the finished piece, the surface of the enamel is flush with the top of the containing walls, which are usually thicker than those in cloisonné work.

Art Nouveau designers adapted motifs from medieval tapestries, Oriental prints, and the drugged dreams of Symbolist poets; among their favorite subjects were animals of all kinds, insects, fantastical creatures, exotic plants, and flowers. Determined to shock or titillate respectable late-Victorian sensibilities, artists like René Lalique, Hector Guimard, and Alphonse Mucha created works that were often flamboyant or erotic.

A fascination with Woman—in her benign or treacherous aspects—dominates much of Art Nouveau jewelry. The ideas of Freud were in the air. Etched in glass, sculpted in gold, or bright with enamel, the era's distinctive madonnas, witches, and nudes appear on cuff links by the Belle Epoque's most prolific designers. Never before or since did so many beguiling ladies adorn men's wrists.

Enamel, amethyst, and 18-carat gold. Tiffany & Co., American, c. 1910. Private Collection

The women's suffrage movement in England and America became increasingly active from 1890 on. Suffragists took green and purple as their colors, which suggests that this pair of links may have belonged to a supporter of the feminist cause.

Emerald and gold mounted on silver. Tiffany & Co., American, c. 1900. Collection Lloyd Macklowe

Eighteen-carat gold with intaglio-carved glass on dark green enamel base, set with diamonds. Lalique, French, 1890s. Collection Lloyd Macklowe

René Lalique (1860–1945) first achieved fame as a jewelry designer in the 1890s. After the turn of the century he began to specialize in art glass, bottles, and industrial packaging for the perfumiers. Lalique was particularly known for his sylphlike nude and seminude figures.

Eighteen-carat-gold beetles. Henri Husson, French,
c. 1900. Private Collection

Gold and blister pearl. American, c. 1900.
Private Collection

Diamond and 18-carat gold. Possibly Marcus & Co.,
American, c. 1900. Private Collection

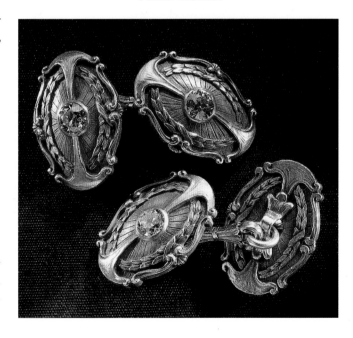

Opposite: Plique-à-jour enamel and gold, set with
diamonds. Probably French, c. 1900. Collection
Lloyd Macklowe

Enamel and silver. Liberty & Co., English, c. 1900. Primavera Gallery, New York

Liberty & Co. was one of the chief sponsors of the British Arts and Crafts movement, producing silver, carpets, pottery, and textiles, as well as jewelry. The interlaced pattern of these links is a Celtic motif particularly associated with Archibald Knox, who designed for Liberty from 1899 to 1912.

Plique-à-jour enamel and 18-carat gold. Designed by Lucien Gaillard, French, c. 1900. Collection Michel Souillac

Chased gold, opal, chalcedony, carnelian, and turquoise dress suite. Designed by Josef Hoffmann for Wiener Werkstätte, Austrian, c. 1910. Private Collection

In 1897 Josef Hoffmann and like-minded Viennese architects banded together to form the first Secession to protest the oppressive official style of the Austrian capital. In 1904 Hoffmann founded the Wiener Werkstätte. Like his contemporaries Henry van de Velde, Hector Guimard, and Charles Rennie Mackintosh, he hoped to bring the aesthetics of high art to daily life.

Gold lotus flowers. Probably American, c. 1900. Private Collection

Gold chimeras. American, 1890s.
James Robinson Inc., New York

Gold. American, c. 1900. Private
Collection

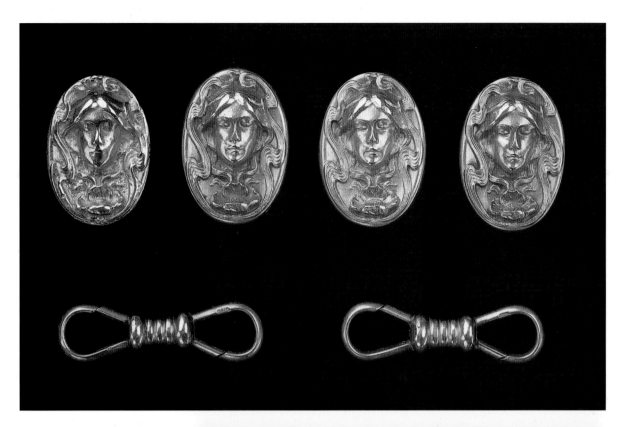

Above: Gold. European, 1890s. Collection Reinhart, Winterthur, Switzerland

The face on the extreme left is a copy made later than the three others.

Gold. American, c. 1900. Private Collection

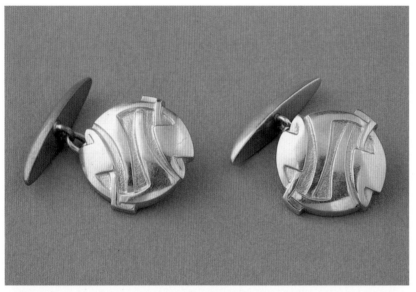

Gold. Designed and owned by Henry van de Velde, Belgian, c. 1900. Gift of Sydney & Frances Lewis, Virginia Museum of Fine Arts, Richmond

Henry van de Velde (1863–1957) was born in Belgium and worked in France and Germany. He was a theorist, architect, and painter. After 1895 he turned his attention to decorative arts, designing furniture, cutlery, and women's clothing. The abstract modernism of his jewelry designs has more in common with German Jugendstil than French or Belgian Art Nouveau.

Eighteen-carat chased gold and cat's-eye. Marcus & Co., American, c. 1900. Collection Neil Lane and Robert Rehnert

Marcus & Co. was founded in 1852 by members of a family who had previous connections with Tiffany & Co. The designers of Marcus were among the first in America to know about and produce pieces in the European Modernist style and among the few American firms in the top ranks of the Arts and Crafts movement.

Silver and moonstone. Probably designed by Georg Jensen, Danish, c. 1905–10. Collection David H. Cohen

Georg Jensen (1866–1935) trained as a goldsmith and worked with silver and pewter in the 1890s, before opening his own firm in 1904. Jensen believed that jewelry should be affordable to the middle class. His pieces sold well but returned little profit. However, by the time William Randolph Hearst bought up the entire Jensen exhibit at the 1915 Panama-Pacific International Exhibition in San Francisco, the jeweler's fame was secure.

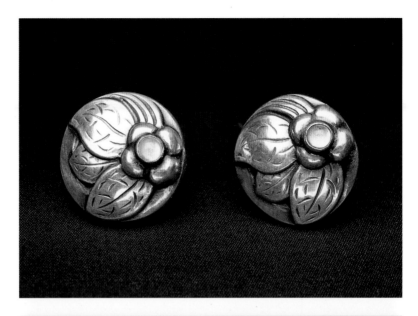

Enamel and gold. American, c. 1910. Private Collection

EDWARDIAN SPLENDOR

Edward, Prince of Wales, 1870s. Photograph made from a plate by Mathew B. Brady

Opposite: White, blue, and *guilloché* red enamel on gold with rubies and diamonds. Fabergé, Russian, c. 1905. Private Collection

The letters ER stand for "Eduardus Rex," Edward VII of Great Britain, to whom these links belonged.

The Fabergé family were the descendants of Huguenot refugees from France who opened a jewelry firm in St. Petersburg in 1842. In 1884 the Empress Maria Feodorovna was given a jeweled egg for Easter, beginning an annual rite of equal importance to the jeweler and the royal family.

Queen Victoria's imperial legacy dominated the reigns of her son, King Edward VII of England, and his cousins Kaiser Wilhelm II of Prussia and Czar Nicholas II of Russia. These monarchs ruled over 400 million subjects around the globe. In Europe before World War I, wealth and prestige remained in the hands of several hundred thousand titled aristocrats who favored the French language, the English hunt, and the Prussian monocle. The Edwardian Age was the last era in which the privileged believed they gave pleasure to the less fortunate by flaunting their wealth in public.

The rich patronized jewelers like Fabergé, Tiffany, and Cartier, who opened branches in every capital and spa to meet the demand. Precious gems—rubies, sapphires, and especially diamonds, alone and in combination with other colored stones—were popular.

By the end of the nineteenth century, the increased availability of Siberian platinum enabled jewelers to create lacelike diamond jewelry that looked deceptively delicate. Much stronger than gold, this "white metal" held stones securely in mounts that were almost invisible. Similarly, the great quantity of South African diamonds stimulated stonecutters to experiment with a variety of shapes. With a ready supply of gems they could afford to be extravagent with material, cutting shallower, more faceted stones to produce greater refraction of light.

The years before World War I saw a revival of dandyism. Dueling flourished, as did eccentricities of dress. Women wore egret feathers and elaborate tiaras. Queen Alexandra of England favored close-fitting, diamond "dog-collar" necklaces, allegedly to cover a small scar on her throat. Her husband, Edward, wore diamonds and rubies at his cuff. Interest in elegant links received a boost with the revival of the turned or "French" cuff.

The pursuit of pleasure led Edwardians and their ladies on an endless social circuit. They traveled to England for the races, to Germany for the waters, and to the French Riviera for the winter sun. By the time of Edward's death in 1910, tensions were rising among the rural poor, the urban proletariat, and Irish and Balkan irredentists. But for the middle and upper classes, in the words of Winston Churchill, "The old world, in its sunset, was fair to see."

Nicholas II and his son, Czarevitch Alexei, in military uniform, October 10, 1915, several years before their murder. A La Vieille Russie, New York

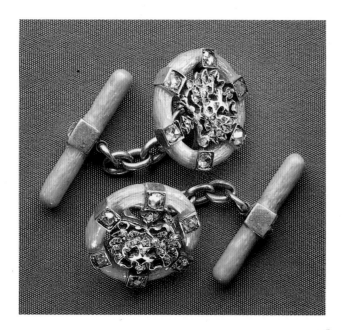

Enamel and rose diamonds. Fabergé, Russian, 1890s. A La Vieille Russie, New York

The double-headed eagle in the center of each link was the emblem of the Romanov family, whose last czar, Nicholas II, was the owner of this pair.

Guilloché blue enamel and gold with diamonds. Fabergé, Russian, 1890s. Collection Baron Alexis de Rédé

These cuff links were originally the property of Czar Alexander III. Though made at the end of the Victorian era, they are similar to pairs made by Fabergé well into the Edwardian period.

Right, above: White enamel on gold with diamonds and rubies. Fabergé, Russian, 1908–15. *Right, below:* Pink enamel and gold. Fabergé, Russian, 1890s. The FORBES Magazine Collection, New York

The pair with anchors and the initial K were made for the Grand Duke Kyrill Vladimirovitch, the first cousin of Nicholas II. They are signed HOLLMING and WIGSTRÖM, respectively, the names of the two most well-known workmasters employed by Fabergé.

Portrait of Cary Grant, 1930s

Gold, diamond, and rubies. Fabergé, Russian, c. 1900. Collection International Gem and Jewelry Show, Inc.

These cuff links were given in 1943 by Barbara Hutton to her third husband, Cary Grant, as a wedding present.

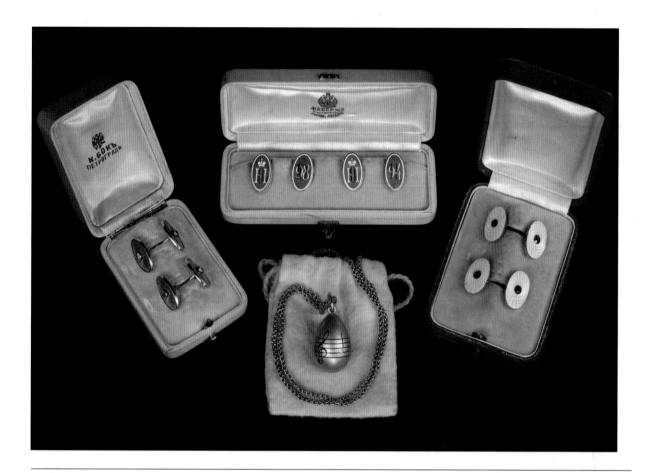

Clockwise from left: Blue enamel on gold, set with diamonds, in fitted original box. Bock of Petrograd, Russian, c. 1915. Emerald and gold, in fitted box, with Cyrillic monogram of the Grand Duchess Olga and dated 1908–14. Fabergé, Russian. White enamel on gold, set with rubies. Astreyden, Russian, c. 1910. Gold Easter egg and chain with diamond. Fabergé, Russian, 1915. Wartski, London

When opened, the egg plays the musical note "A," for Grand Duchess Anastasia, to whom the egg belonged.

These four items were carried out of Russia by Charles Sydney Gibbs, the tutor to the royal children, whom Nicholas and Alexandra had hired in 1908 at the suggestion of their cousin Edward VII. Gibbs returned to England after the family was killed at Ekaterinburg and was subsequently ordained as a Russian Orthodox priest.

Guilloché red enamel on gold. Child & Child, English, c. 1900. Private Collection

White and *guilloché* blue enamel on gold. Probably English, c. 1905. Collection Norton Rosenbaum

The radiating, engine-turned *guilloché* engraving under the blue enamel is one of the most characteristic designs of Edwardian jewelry.

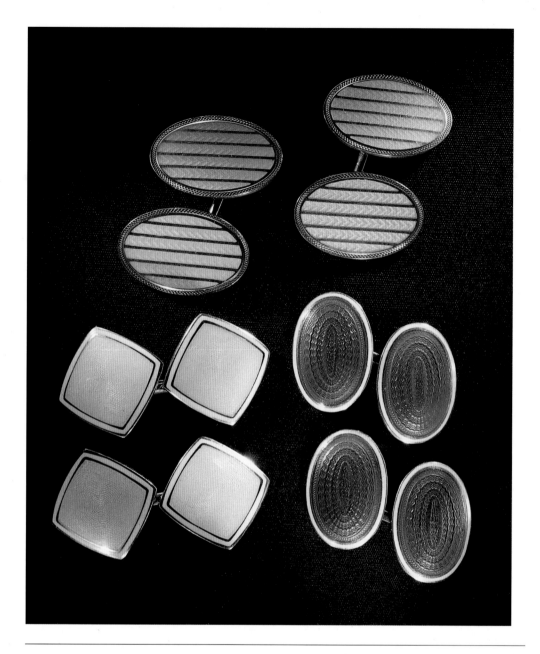

Top: *Guilloché* enamel on gold. Carter, Howe & Co., American, c. 1910–15. *Lower left: Guilloché* enamel and 14-carat gold. Carrington & Co., American, 1910–15. *Lower right: Guilloché* enamel and 15-carat gold. English, c. 1915. Private Collection

Guilloché enameling—a process of laying translucent enamel over an engine-turned ground—was a secret of Fabergé's craftsmen, only later mastered by other jewelers.

These links were all made just before World War I. The style of engraving under the enamel is more elaborate than that of an earlier day and anticipates the Art Deco style.

Enamel, natural pearls, and gold. French, c. 1900–1905. Private Collection

Platinum and 18-carat gold. English, c. 1910. D. S. Lavender, London

Although it would replace gold as the most popular setting for gemstones in the 1920s, platinum was first used only in conjunction with other metals.

Fashion illustration of an Edwardian gentleman dressed for dinner. From *La Mode,* 1912. Union Française des Arts du Costume

White and *guilloché* pink enamel on gold. Cartier, French, 1910. Cartier Collection

Enamel on gold. Chaumet, French, 1910. Chaumet Museum

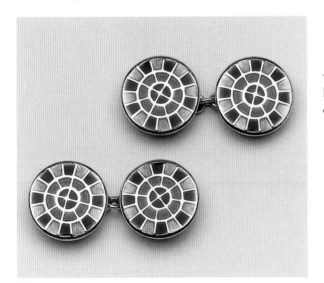

Fashion illustration of an Edwardian gentleman dressed for a summer outing. From *La Mode*, 1912. Union Française des Arts du Costume

Sapphires, diamonds, and platinum. European, c. 1910–20. Private Collection

These cuff links anticipate the Art Deco period in the flamboyance of the design and the delicacy of the setting.

Cabochon rubies, diamonds, and platinum. European, c. 1910–20. Private Collection

Ruby, Oriental pearl, diamonds, and gold dress suite. French, c. 1910. Private Collection

ART DECO:
Jazz and Geometry

Fashion illustration of a Jazz Age gentleman on the town. From *Maîtres-Tailleurs de Paris*, Summer 1922. Union Française des Arts du Costume

Opposite: Lapis lazuli and diamonds. European, 1930s. Collection Edward H. Merrin

An Englishman, recalling Paris in the 1920s, said that the hot topics of conversation were "Cubist and other queer paintings . . . typewriters . . . cocaine . . . silk stockings . . . Freudism . . . unnatural vices . . . aeroplanes and cocktails."

In the years following World War I, national, social, and moral boundaries were in flux. The avant-garde embraced anything new, fast, or subversive. Stimulated by ideas from modern art, particularly the geometric abstractions of Cubism, designers in Europe and America created graphics, furnishings, and jewelry that looked at the world from new perspectives. At the 1925 Exposition des Arts Décoratifs et Industriels Modernes in Paris—which gave Art Deco its name—they set out to prove that art and industry together could set the tone for living in the modern age.

A cultivated informality marked both the new social order and fashion. The nineteenth-century gentleman's daytime uniform of top hat and tailcoat or morning suit survived only as formal wear. Yet the stylish man never left home without his gold Dunhill lighter, his platinum and onyx Van Cleef & Arpels cigarette case, his Cartier tank watch, and his crisply striped blue-and-white-enamel cuff links.

In the 1920s and 1930s, long-established jewelry firms like Cartier, Boucheron, Chaumet, Mellerio, and Van

Cleef & Arpels developed an increasingly symbiotic relationship with the haute couture. The Cartier family intermarried with the fashion house of Worth. The wife of jeweler René Boivin was a sister of dress designer Paul Poiret. Coco Chanel and Elsa Schiaparelli helped launch the careers of jewelry designers Fulco di Verdura and Jean Schlumberger.

Art Deco jewelers worked with materials ranging from traditional precious stones to the unorthodox or innovative—plastics, chrome, and steel. Platinum, growing in popularity since the beginning of the century, turned out to be a lustrous complement to coral, jade, and lapis, which were all the rage. Along with white gold, platinum was prized for its "neutral lunar glow."

The jewelers of the Art Deco period created cuff links whose geometric clarity and bold use of color continue to be particularly appealing to contemporary tastes. The quintessential Deco combination of platinum, diamonds, and onyx remains the dress suite of choice for many a well-dressed man.

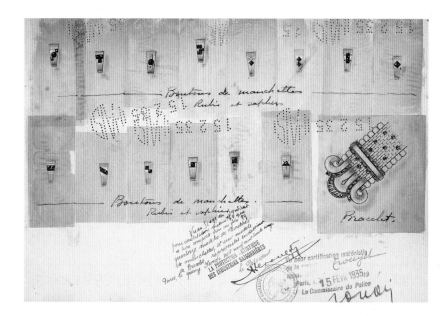

Design page from Van Cleef & Arpels, Paris. 1934

The stamp from the Commissioner of Police is an indication of copyright protection.

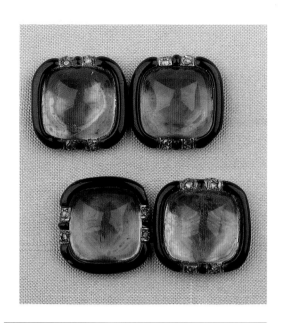

Topaz, diamonds, and onyx on gold. René Boivin, French, 1920s. Collection Prince Jean-Louis de Faucigny-Lucinge

Enamel and gold. French, 1920s. Private Collection

Enamel on platinum. Designed by Raymond Templier, French, 1920s. Collection Michel Souillac

Raymond Templier, a founding member of the Union of Modern Artists, made jewelry and cigarette cases. He was fond of black and white, pairing precious white metals—platinum and silver—with onyx or other dark stones.

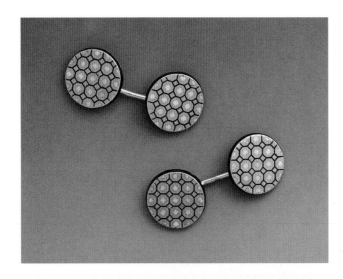

Ivory and black enamel on gold. Cartier, French, 1929. Private Collection

Platinum with square cabochon sapphires and enamel. Cartier, French, 1928. Private Collection

This pair was originally owned by Baron Eugène de Rothschild.

Onyx set with diamonds. Cartier, French, 1925. Private Collection

The diamonds form the Chinese sign for happiness, a popular motif in the 1920s and 1930s.

Onyx, diamonds, and rubies. French, 1920. Private Collection

Diamond and ruby dress suite. French, 1930s. Private Collection

Platinum, onyx, and diamonds. Designed by Raymond Templier, French, 1920s. Primavera Gallery, New York

Dress suite of crystal inlaid with onyx and rose diamonds. French, c. 1930. Private Collection

Platinum with inlaid enamel and rose diamonds. Cartier, French, 1920. Collection Fred Leighton

Jade, onyx, and diamonds. French, 1920s. Private Collection

Sapphires and diamonds on matte platinum. French, c. 1930. Private Collection

Designed to look three dimensional, the faces of these links are perfectly flat.

Painted ivory. Designed by Clément Mère, French, 1920s. Collection Michel Souillac

Clément Mère, who trained as a painter, worked for several fashion houses. He achieved his greatest acclaim as a furniture designer. The style of decoration on these links appears on many of his large pieces.

Platinum, horn, and onyx. Chaumet, French, 1929. Chaumet Museum

Enamel on platinum. Designed by Jean Dunand, French, 1920s. Collection Michel Souillac

Jean Dunand, who began his career as a sculptor, is well known for his metal and lacquer vases and lacquer furniture and screens. Red, black, and silver form his signature color scheme.

Platinum with watch. Cartier, French, 1938. Cartier Museum

The wristwatch was invented by Cartier in 1904 and became very popular as a result of World War I. The watch face on these cuff links is a classic Cartier design.

Three individual links of silver and Bohemian garnets. Designed by Rudolf Stockar for the Artěl Cooperative, Prague, 1920s. Museum of Decorative Arts, Prague

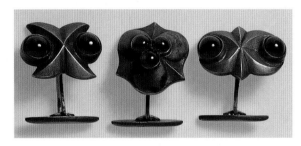

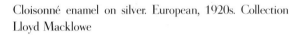

Fashion illustration of a gentleman dressed for the day's affairs. From *Maîtres-Tailleurs de Paris,* Summer 1922. Union Française des Arts du Costume

Cloisonné enamel on silver. European, 1920s. Collection Lloyd Macklowe

Above: Gold inlaid with lapis lazuli. Ostertag, French, 1920s. Collection A. S. G.

Gold. Designed by Paul Brandt, French, 1930s. Collection Michel Souillac

White and *guilloché* blue enamel on gold. 1920s. Collection Edward H. Merrin

Eighteen-carat white and yellow gold. French, early 1930s. Primavera Gallery, New York

Enamel and silver with vermeil finish. American, c. 1925. Collection Lloyd Macklowe

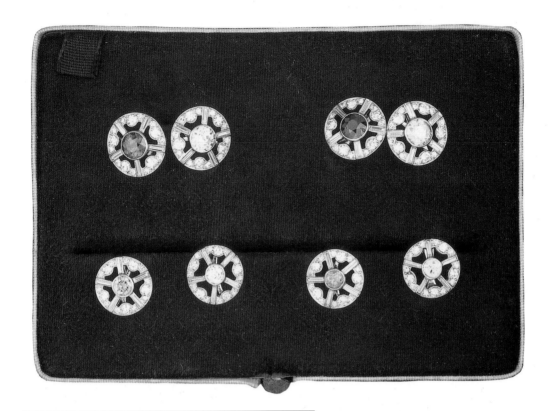

Fancy-colored diamond and diamond dress suite. French, 1924. Collection Van Cleef & Arpels

This pair was made by Van Cleef & Arpels for Count Guy du Boisrouvray, a French mining engineer who was married to a member of the Bolivian Patiño family.

Portrait of Count Guy du Boisrouvray, 1937

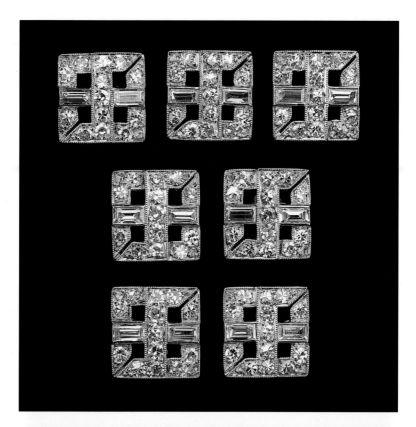

Diamonds and platinum. Chaumet, French, 1930. Private Collection

Diamond and platinum dress suite. Lacloche, French, 1930s. Private Collection

THE SPORTING LIFE

There was once a time before polo shirts, when men wore waistcoats, cravats, starched shirts, and cuff links to ride, shoot, or play golf. In *The Old Wives' Tale* (1908), Arnold Bennett described an aspect of a turn-of-the-century character's sporting dress: "An essential portion of the man's braces, visible sometimes when he played at tennis, consisted of chain, and the upper and nether halves of his cuff links were connected by chains." From the turn of the century on, the country weekend was a fixture of upper-class society. With proper clothes prescribed for shooting, polo, croquet, golf, or just lolling about, a gentleman could change his costume seven times before dinner. The Paris *Herald* reported in 1902, "Sporting tastes have so invaded modern society that a fashion paper dealing exclusively with sporting costumes might sustain the interest of its weekly readers from one end of the year to the other."

Country clothes were adopted for town wear, just as sneakers and jogging suits appeared on city streets in the 1980s. The trendsetter in the sporting look was the Duke of Windsor who, as Prince of Wales, could be seen on the golf course wearing short baggy knee breeches called plus fours, a tweed cap with a flat crown, and a Fair Isle sweater.

Since the Victorian era, hunting and fishing scenes or portraits of animals have been among the most popular

Enamel on gold, set with rose diamonds and rubies. Possibly by Chaumet, French, 1920s. Collection Michel Souillac cuff links for sportswear. Sometimes these are enameled on gold discs, or they may be painted under so-called reverse crystals. In these links, the outline of design is incised, upside down and backwards, on the flat underside of a cabochon, or domed, unfaceted crystal. The picture is then painted in, the tiniest detail sometimes requiring a brush with only one bristle. Finally, the crystal is mounted on a backing of mother-of-pearl. When the link is worn, the painted image appears to be floating inside the crystal.

In 1935 reverse-crystal links were called by *Men's Wear* "an almost perfect and a most flexible medium for expressing the sport idea in jewelry. There is something clean, cool and clear—and yet colorful—about crystals that keeps the imagination of the real sportsman stimulated. And they are lovely to look at, from the cheap little fifty-centers up to the finest hand-cut and colored stones in the swankest jeweler on the Avenue."

Men no longer wear sporting jewelry in the paddock or on the golf course, but they have always felt comfortable with sporting motifs on their neckties, tie clips, and cuff links. As *Men's Wear* pointed out in September 1934: "The men who buy know nothing of horses, dogs, guns, boats, and polo mallets. They may have a bowing acquaintance with tennis racquets and golf clubs, but they are not sportsmen in the accepted sense. They simply need an excuse for jewelry."

Fashion illustration of gentlemen dressed for a day at the golf club. From *Maîtres-Tailleurs de Paris*, Summer 1922. Union Française des Arts du Costume

Four different fishing flies, under cabochon crystals, and white gold. René Boivin, French, c. 1910. Collection René Boivin

Reverse-crystal intaglio enamel on gold. American, 1925. James Robinson Inc., New York

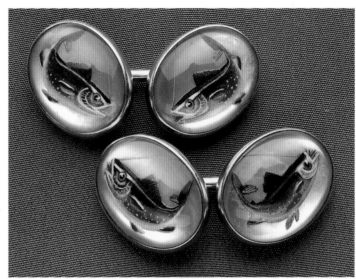

Reverse-crystal intaglio enamel on gold. Cartier, American, c. 1910. James Robinson Inc., New York

Enamel on gold. Goldsmiths & Silversmiths Co., English, 1925. James Robinson Inc., New York

Carved inlaid mother-of-pearl on gold. J. E. Caldwell & Co., American, c. 1930. Private Collection

Fashion illustration of gentlemen dressed for a day of shooting. From *Maîtres-Tailleurs de Paris*, Winter 1922–23. Union Française des Arts du Costume

Gold and enamel. English, 1990. Hancocks & Co., London

Shades-of-gold hunting horns. English, c. 1880. A La Vieille Russie, New York

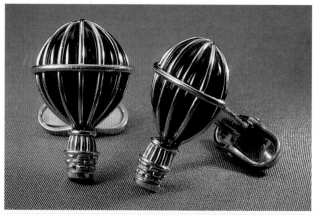

Eighteen-carat gold and onyx. Van Cleef & Arpels, New York, 1984. Collection the late Malcolm Forbes

This pair was a gift to the well-known publisher and balloon fancier from his wife.

Emeralds and gold. European, probably 1920s. Collection Edward H. Merrin

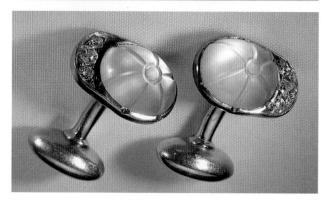

Moonstone, rose diamond, and gold jockey caps. English, late 19th century. A La Vieille Russie, New York

Four hunting scenes in platinum and gold. Cartier, New York, 1930s. Private Collection

Emeralds and gold. Hermès, French, late 1930s. Collection Jay Spectre

A FANCIFUL MENAGERIE

Gold, enamel, diamonds, and emeralds. Designed by Gene Moore for Tiffany & Co., American, 1980s. Collection the late Stuart Jacobson

---

Opposite: Enamel and gold with diamonds. American, 1945–50. Private Collection

gyptians carried carved scarab amulets to ward off death. Native American clans often took the names of predatory animals. European kings have been associated with animal avatars: François I of France took the salamander as his emblem, Louis XII adopted the hedgehog, and Richard I of England was called the "Lion-Hearted."

The Royal Society for Protection Against Cruelty to Animals was founded in England in 1824, sixty years before the Society for the Prevention of Cruelty to Children. The first Paris Dog Show took place in 1877. The American Cat Association was founded in 1897. Victorians were serious about their pets.

When Victorian designers ransacked archaeology for unusual animal motifs, they rediscovered the scarab. Other unsavory insects, such as the horsefly, wood louse, and earwig, were the subjects of elaborate jewels. Bees, the emblem of the Bonaparte family, had a vogue in the 1850s and 1860s in honor of Emperor Napoleon III.

Different jeweled species have been popular at different times. Tiny animals made of semiprecious stones were a favorite gift of the Russian nobility. Pierre Cartier came home from a trip to St. Petersburg with an alabaster hen and a purpurin toad. Before long his own workshops were turning out piglets, elephants, and foxes of ivory, gold, or jade. Dragonflies and butterflies were popular with Art Nouveau designers. Twentieth-century jewelers have produced coral ladybugs, gold starfish, and diamond seahorses.

Cats have always been in favor. Panthers were a sort of totem animal for Jeanne Toussaint, the intimate companion of Louis Cartier. Toussaint, who decorated her Paris apartment with panther skins, allegedly was called "the panther" by Mr. Cartier. From the time she became head of Cartier's Haute Joaillerie in 1933, the firm made a specialty of cat jewelry. Diamond and onyx panthers lolled, stalked, and pounced; their emerald or sapphire eyes tracked the comings and goings of owners like the Duchess of Windsor, Barbara Hutton, and the Princess Sadruddin Aga Khan.

In postwar America the expatriate Italian nobleman Fulco di Verdura created a fanciful menagerie on brooches, bracelets, and cuff links. His distinctive animals, in witty combinations of enamel, stone, and gold, have influenced the design of popular links ever since.

Enamel on gold with emeralds. Cartier, French, 1960s. Collection Leonard Stanley

Lapis lazuli and 18-carat gold with cabochon sapphire and diamonds. Verdura, American, 1950s. Collection Leonard Stanley

Fulco di Verdura (1898–1978), a Sicilian nobleman, was a cousin of Giuseppe di Lampedusa, the author of *The Leopard*. Verdura moved to Paris in the 1920s and became the head jewelry designer for Coco Chanel. He was always inventive; while platinum and diamonds were still the rage, he was experimenting with gold and colored stones. He moved to America in 1934, where he first worked as a designer for Paul Flato before establishing his own firm in New York in 1939.

Eighteen-carat gold and sapphires. JAR, Paris, 1980s. Private Collection

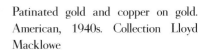

Patinated gold and copper on gold. American, 1940s. Collection Lloyd Macklowe

These beetle shapes are Japanese sword-hilt ornaments, probably from the 1880s, which were made into cuff links at a later date.

Freshwater pearl and gold. American, c. 1900. Collection Neil Lane and Robert Rehnert

Ivory and gold with sapphires. Made in France for Tiffany & Co., 1950s. Private Collection

Sapphires with gold mountain lions. 1930s. Private Collection

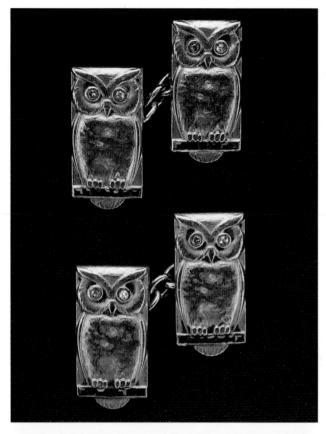

Gold with rubies and diamonds. Vever, French, 1900. Collection Fred Leighton

The Vever brothers, Paul and Henri, were well-known Parisian jewelers specializing in Art Nouveau designs. Henri also produced a three-volume history of French jewelry of the nineteenth century.

These links are missing several stones because their owner wears them almost every day.

Enamel, gold, and rubies. David Webb, American, 1970s. David Webb Inc., New York

Enamel, gold, and cabochon rubies. David Webb, American, 1980s. Collection John M. Davis

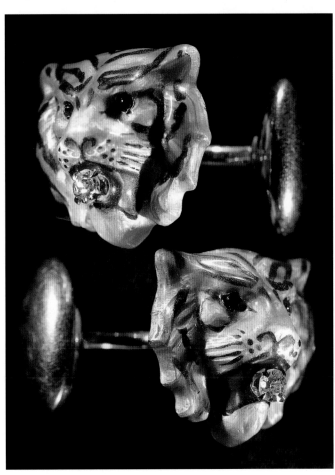

Enamel and gold with diamonds. American, c. 1900. Private Collection

PERSONAL WHIMSIES

Whimsical cuff links reveal something about the man who wears them. He has chosen to display—discreetly but decisively—his profession, his passion, or his sense of humor. The jewelers at David Webb remember fondly the special order for a complete dress suite of enameled chickens from a customer who was proud to show the world he was a pillar of the poultry trade. An oil man wears platinum derricks. A romantic wife orders her husband a set of gold pigs, explaining that the reference is to their private "love code."

Cartier has made at least one pair of links from a tooth supplied by a customer. Verdura wrapped a client's gallstones in gold. In 1939 a Parisian jeweler filled a German official's order for onyx and diamond swastikas.

Novelties need not be one of a kind. Jewelers will make a set of links marking a man's birthday on a gold calendar. Brokers can order bulls and bears. Eyes with a teardrop have been made since Victorian times, when they were sometimes worn as mourning jewelry. Motifs an earlier age thought were naughty—the four vices, playing cards, a whiskey glass, or a lit cigar—continue to be popular today.

Silkscreen image with overglaze on porcelain. Designed by Piero Fornasetti, Italian, 1950s. Collection Martin Eidelberg

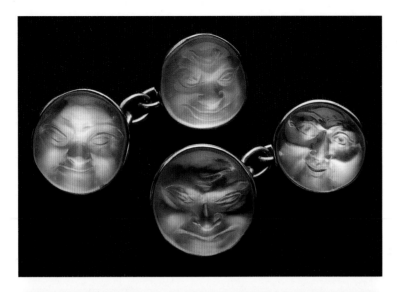

Hand-carved moonstones and white gold. European, 1920s. Private Collection

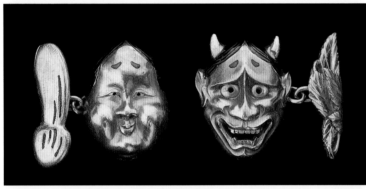

Enamel and white and yellow gold. French, probably 1930s. Collection Michel Souillac

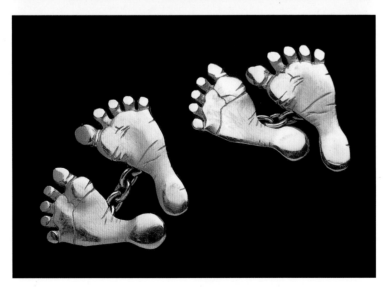

Platinum. Paul Flato, American, c. 1940. Collection Leonard Stanley

These links belonged originally to Adrian, the noted Hollywood costume designer.

Upper left: Glass doll's eye, platinum teardrop, and gold. *Middle:* Eighteen-carat gold. *All others:* Eighteen-carat gold and oxidized silver. All designed by Louis Féron for Bronzini, New York, 1950s

Louis Féron, who trained as a sculptor and a goldsmith, fled European fascism in the 1930s and later helped organize a group of Free French sympathizers in Central America. In 1945 Féron moved to New York, where he worked with fellow refugee Jean Schlumberger to create jewelry and accessories, mostly for Tiffany & Co. In his own name, Féron made women's jewelry for Tiffany & Co. and men's jewelry for Bronzini in the 1950s and 1960s.

Enamel on silver, gold, and steel. English, 1914–18.
Collection A. S. G.

Coral, lapis lazuli, cabochon sapphires, and gold. Bulgari, American, 1976. Collection Jay Spectre

Gold, platinum, and pearl. Tiffany & Co., American, c. 1900. Private Collection

Enamel on gold. English, 1920s. Tender Buttons, New York

Twenty-two-carat gold and steel. Daniel Brush, American, 1990. Private Collection

Gold. American, 1960s. Collection Brooke Shields

Eighteen-carat gold and cabochon emerald. Mellerio, French, c. 1935. Lewis M. Kaplan Associates, Ltd., London

This stylish pair may show a waiter carrying a cocktail tray, a smoker with a very large cigar, or a gangster with a submachine gun.

Eighteen-carat gold and opals. Kevin Coates, London, 1987. Collection the late Stuart Jacobson

Intrigued with the legend of Icarus, the owner commissioned a London artist-goldsmith to create these links. The figure on the left shows Icarus rising toward the sun, represented by a fire opal set in gold flames. The right-hand link depicts Icarus falling into the sea, represented by a water opal set in gold waves.

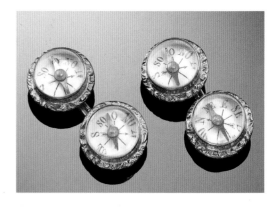

Compasses under crystal set in embossed gold. European, c. 1860. Courtesy Sotheby's, London

This pair is said to have belonged to Emperor Maximilian of Mexico, the brother of Emperor Franz Josef of Austria. Maximilian was supposedly wearing them when he was shot in Querétaro in 1867 at the end of his ill-fated attempt to overthrow the democracy of Benito Juarez.

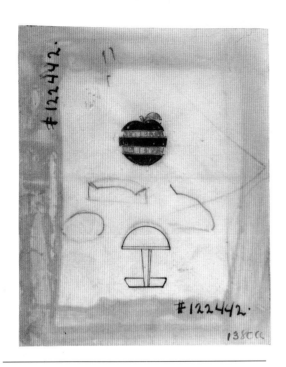

Cuff-link design by Oscar Heyman & Brothers, Inc., 1940s. Oscar Heyman Archives, New York

Enamel, diamonds, and gold. Verdura, American, 1990. Verdura Collection

This pair, one representing the globe in daylight and the other the starry night sky, was inspired by Cole Porter's signature ballad, *Night and Day*. The original pair was designed by Verdura for Porter in 1941.

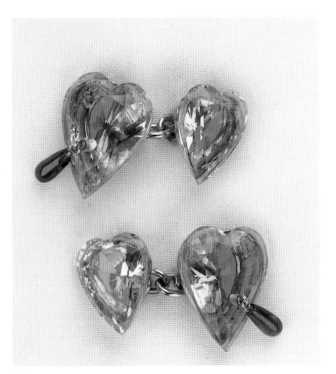

Aquamarine and ruby. Cartier, French, 1975. Private Collection

Emeralds, diamonds, and gold. Designed by James Pendleton, made by René Boivin, French, 1950. Collection James Pendleton

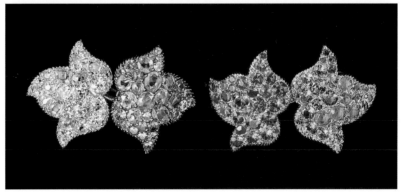

Diamonds and colored stones. JAR, Paris, 1989. Collection Donald Drabkin

ACKNOWLEDGMENTS

The idea for a book on cuff links originated with the late Stuart Jacobson. We are indebted to him for his imagination and to his parents, Ruth and Coleman Jacobson, for their commitment to his vision.

At the outset of the project, we sought guidance from various jewelry and costume specialists. Joyce Jonas gave us access to her extensive library and answered every question with expertise and enthusiasm. Geoffrey Munn at Wartski; Robert Kaufmann at the Metropolitan Museum Costume Institute Library; Ilene Chazanof; Janet Zapata at the Tiffany Archives; Edward Munves and Kim Harwood at James Robinson; Ralph Esmerian; Ralph Destino at Cartier; and Peter Schaffer at A La Vieille Russie were generous with their time and advice and we thank them. We also thank Charles Mikolaycak, who helped us imagine what a book devoted to cuff links might look like.

In London Edwin and Carol Taylor made available the Pym family archives and arranged to have various pieces photographed; we owe them our gratitude. In addition, Jonathan Condrup at Sotheby's; David Callaghan at Hancocks; Teresa Buxton at the Cartier Archives; Jill Spanner and Tessa Murdoch at the Museum of London; Richard Edgcomb, Avril Hart, and Janet Markarian at the Victoria and Albert Museum; B. E. Norman at Harvey & Gore; and Simon Teakle at Christie's freely gave assistance, as did Malcolm Carr at Hamilton and Inches in Edinburgh.

In Paris Joel Rosenthal and Pierre Jeannet of JAR led us to new sources for unusual links and also helped expedite the photography. Our assistant, Agathe Berman, arranged important appointments and followed up every lead. We especially thank Philippe Bessis at Cartier; Betty Jais at the Cartier Archives; Michel de Robert at Mauboussin; Béatrice de Plinval at Chaumet; François Canavy at Van Cleef & Arpels; Fabienne Falluel at the Musée de la Mode et du Costume; Florence Müller at the Union Française des Arts du Costume; Anne-Marie Colban at Charvet; Daniel Rouzières at René Boivin; Sir Valentine Abdy; and Count Brando Brandolini.

From Münster, Germany, Professor Kurt Tetzeli von Rosador sent valuable advice about literary references to jewelry. Dr. Věra Vokáčová of the Museum of Decorative Arts in Prague sent material about her collection.

Our gratitude extends to all the collectors and jewelers who shared their knowledge and passion for cuff links with us, particularly Daniel Brush; Barbara Macklowe at Macklowe Gallery and Modernism; Marilyn Meyers at Asprey; Jay Spectre; Diana Epstein and Millicent Safro at Tender Buttons; Rosario Schwan at Louis Féron; Alan Graham; Richard Polsky; Norton Rosenbaum; Brian Albert; Joe Ahumado; Horst; Valentine Lawford; Leonard Stanley; James Pendleton; Neil Lane and Robert Rehnert; Holton Roher; Ellen Israel and Marcie Imberman at Kentshire Galleries; Haim Manishevitz and Audrey Friedman at Primavera; and Edward Landrigan at Verdura.

We also wish to thank Rose Casella at A La Vieille Russie; Jean Cohen at N. W. Ayer; Meredith Nieves at Jay Spectre; Jimi Napoli at Palazzetti; Susan Morganstern at Tender Buttons; Michael Berna at Primavera; Margaret Kelly at The Forbes Magazine Collection; Lillian Ostergard at Verdura; Liz Gabor at The Alexander and Louisa Calder Foundation; Jacqueline Fay at Sotheby's, New York; Carol Elkins at Sotheby's West; Bernard Berger at Sotheby's, Geneva; Ronald Brenne at the Bettman Archive; Alan H. Rabinovich at Oscar Heyman and Brothers; Shawn Berg at Lewis M. Kaplan Associates, London; Patricia Ferenczi and Maria Mato at Christie's, New York; Glynn Valentine at Tiffany & Co.; and Joel Rothschild.

To Kenneth Williams and Donald Amor of Turnbull and Asser we owe special thanks for providing shirting to serve as backdrops for most of the photographs in the book.

We thank the photographers whose work is represented, especially John Parnell, Katharina Tucci, and Jennifer Cheung. We also thank Martha Bardach at *Time* magazine for her photographic guidance and Carole Kismaric and Hugh Nissenson for their astute comments on the text.

This publication would not have been possible without the support of Paul Gottlieb, the editorial skill of Harriet Whelchel, and the design direction of Carol Robson.

INDEX

Page numbers listed in *italics* refer to illustrations and captions.

PHOTOGRAPH CREDITS

All photographs are by John Parnell, with the following exceptions:

A. C. COOPER LTD., London: 9, 48 bottom right. A LA VIEILLE RUSSIE, courtesy of: 42 top. ALLEN, JIM: 75, 88 bottom left. BETTMANN: 41. BOISROUVRAY, ALBINA DU, courtesy of: 64 bottom. CARTIER INTERNATIONAL, Paris, courtesy of: 7, 13, 25 left, 49 top left, 56, 61 top, 94 top, 96 bottom. CHAUMET, Paris, courtesy of: 49 bottom, 60 middle. CHEUNG, JENNIFER: 16, 38 bottom, 76, 77 top, 78 bottom, 84 bottom, 104 bottom, 109 top. CLETO MUNARI DESIGN ASSOCIATI, Vicenza, courtesy of: 105 bottom. COLORWORKS, INC. © 1990: 44 bottom, 92 bottom right. DAVID WEBB, INC., courtesy of: 80 bottom. DONOHOE, London: 10 top. FELICIANO, courtesy The FORBES Magazine Collection: 43 bottom. HAMILTON & INCHES LTD., Edinburgh, courtesy of: 26 bottom. HANCOCKS & CO. LTD., London, courtesy of: 25 upper right, 27 top, 71 top. HARVEY & GORE, London, courtesy of: 11 top. HASESCHMUNDT, DR. ULRIKE VON, courtesy of: 35 top. HEARST CORPORATION, copyright © 1937. Courtesy *Harper's Bazaar* and Bettman: 8. HORST: 98 left. JONAS, JOYCE, courtesy of: 23 bottom right. KOBAL COLLECTION/ SUPERSTOCK: 44 top, 93. MUSEUM OF DECORATIVE ARTS, Prague, courtesy of: 61 middle. MUSEUM OF LONDON: 10 bottom, 11 bottom. OSCAR HEYMAN & BROTHERS, INC., courtesy of: 89 top left. PRUDENCE CUMING ASSOCIATES LTD., London: 88 top. RENÉ BOIVIN, Paris, courtesy of: 68 bottom. ROSS, JACK R.: 39 top, 103 top. S. J. PHILLIPS LTD., London, courtesy of: 22 bottom right. SOTHEBY'S, London, courtesy of: 88 bottom right. TIFFANY ARCHIVES, courtesy of: 29. TUCCI, KATHARINA: 33 top left, 34 bottom, 37 top, 43 top, 50, 55 top left and bottom, 60 top and bottom, 62 top left, 65 top, 66, 77 bottom, 84 middle, 89 bottom, 108, 109 bottom. UFAC, Paris: 48 left, 49 right, 53, 61 bottom left, 68 top, 70 bottom. VAN CLEEF & ARPELS, Paris, courtesy of: 2, 54, 64 top. VERDURA, courtesy of: 89 top right, 98 right, 99 top. VIRGINIA MUSEUM OF FINE ARTS: 38 top. WARTSKI, London, courtesy of: 21, 24 top, 45.